NUMEROLOGY

NUMEROLOGY

Sahar Huneidi Palmer

Images courtesy of Shutterstock.

This edition published in 2024 by Arcturus Publishing Limited
26/27 Bickels Yard, 151–153 Bermondsey Street,
London SE1 3HA

Copyright © Arcturus Holdings Limited

All rights reserved. No part of this publication may be reproduced, stored in a retrieval system, or transmitted, in any form or by any means, electronic, mechanical, photocopying, recording or otherwise, without prior written permission in accordance with the provisions of the Copyright Act 1956 (as amended). Any person or persons who do any unauthorised act in relation to this publication may be liable to criminal prosecution and civil claims for damages.

AD011740UK

Printed in China

Contents

Introduction 6

Chapter One
The Vibrations of Numbers 8

Chapter Two
Numerological Interpretations 50

Chapter Three
Numerology Readings 116

Further Reading 128

Introduction

*Three is the number of those who do holy work;
Two is the number of those who do lover's work;
One is the number of those who do perfect
evil or perfect good.*

– American Novelist Clive Barker, from *Abarat*

INTRODUCTION

Harry Potter's friend, Hermione Granger, gives 'arithmancy' as her favourite subject at their magical school. The novel demonstrates that arithmancy involves the supernatural qualities of numbers as Hermione learns to use intricate numerological charts to perform divinations. In the real world, arithmancy is referred to as numerology.

Numerology is the study of the relationship between numbers and various elements of the world we live in. Numerology encapsulates the numerical significance of letters in words or names, numbers which form the date of birth, ideas and concepts. Many new-age practitioners refer to objects like crystals, gemstones, colours, and essential oils as having a vibration. Numerology is concerned with the mystical meaning of numbers by interpreting their inherent 'vibration', or unique qualities. This interpretation is derived from a person's date of birth or letters composing their name and can inspire significant insights into how to fulfil their life purpose.

With the card deck accompanying this book, you can begin to tune into the vibrations of numbers and discover what each number indicates for you and your destiny. Whether used as an oracle to predict the future or simply to inform you about what influences sit behind a decision or dilemma, this can be a useful tool for greater understanding of the world around you – and your place in it.

CHAPTER 1
The Vibrations of Numbers

CHAPTER 1

Before 1907, the term 'numerology' did not exist in the English language. However, as early as 500 BCE, the philosophers of the ancient Classical Greek world – such as Pythagoras, Aristotle, and Plato – were eager to unravel the mysteries of our universe by expressing the interrelationships between various elements and objects in the natural world, the seasons, the planets and sound, and through numbers, equations, and symbols.

Moreover, Pythagoras and his pupils believed that numbers possessed mystical qualities. They thought that numbers were the foundation of the universe, which operated on numerical harmony. In *Numerology: Or What Pythagoras Wrought* (Cambridge University Press, 1997), author Underwood Dudley writes that Pythagoreans – the followers of Pythagoras – developed an interest in number mysticism after learning this really intriguing truth about numbers: Any combination of odd integers that starts with 1 will always produce a square number.

St. Augustine of Hippo (354–430 CE), theologian, philosopher and bishop of Hippo Regius in Numidia, Roman North Africa, was also a Pythagorean. His mysticism-related publications had an impact on the growth of Western philosophy and Western Christianity. He had the same view as Pythagoras, which was that everything had numerical links, and it was up to the mind to explore and examine the 'secrets of these relationships or have them revealed by divine grace.'

Around one of his major works, *Metaphysics*, written in 350 BCE, Aristotle made the claim that 'The so-called Pythagoreans, who were the first to take up mathematics, not only advanced this subject but saturated with it, they fancied that the principles of mathematics were the principles of all things.'

Pythagoras originally identified correlations between musical notes and numbers in order to mathematically explain the vibration of string instruments. Most likely, the concept of numbers having vibrations and properties began here. Pythagoras discovered that the pitch of a musical note is proportional to the length of the string that creates it, and that intervals between harmonic sound frequencies form simple numerical ratios.

The Pythagoreans, who came afterwards, employed numbers to correlate a person's name and date of birth to

CHAPTER 1

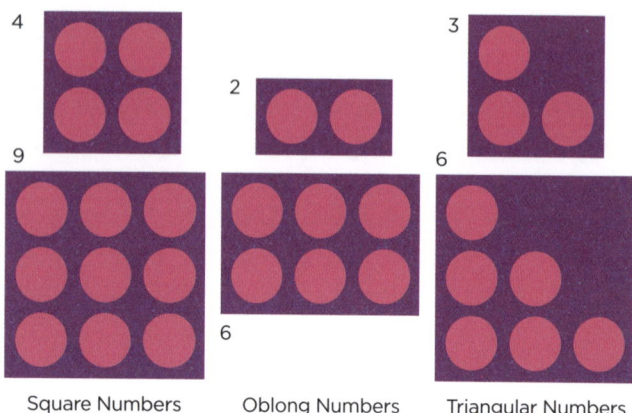

Square Pythagorean Triangle and Rectangle Numbers

indicate that person's outer character or personality. Moreover, the Pythagoreans categorized numbers by the shape of the arrangement formed. Since a certain number of dots, or pebbles, can be arranged in a perfect square, numbers like 1, 4, and 9 were thought of 'square' numbers.

In addition, numbers 1, 3, 6 and 10 were 'triangle' numbers because one, three and six or ten dots or pebbles can be arranged to form a triangle. And numbers 2, 6, and 12 are thought of as 'rectangle' numbers since they can be arranged in the shape of a triangle (see above).

In addition to describing numbers in terms of math and geometry (see opposite), Pythagoreans also described numbers in term of their **non-numerical** properties. The latter had to do with intuition and mysticism more than mathematics. For instance, **even** numbers were **feminine**, whereas **odd numbers** were **masculine**.

Specific numbers have mystical characteristics in Pythagorean numerology. Because all other numbers can be formed by adding 1, the number **1** symbolized oneness, the genesis of all things. The number **1** has come to represent harmony, the beginning of everything. Furthermore, **1** also symbolized creativity, since adding any number to it creates more numbers.

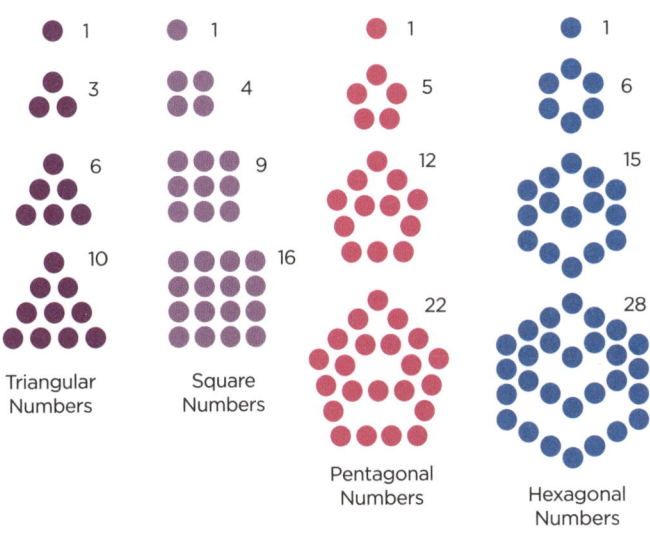

Polygonal Numbers

THE VIBRATIONS OF NUMBERS

Geometry and Numerology

Around 400 BCE, Plato discovered a relationship between the five platonic solids and the four elements of nature. This lead him to their classification as cosmic solids. The cube symbolizes the **earth**, the octahedron symbolizes the **air**, the tetrahedron symbolizes **fire**, the icosahedron symbolizes **water**, and the dodecahedron was supposed to be the element that 'made up the heavens', symbolizing the **cosmos**, or the universe. These five main shapes became known as The Platonic Solids. The Platonic solids are unique in that they represent every possible molecular link or geometric structure that exits in nature. As a result, to the ancient Greeks they represented the foundation of all physical matter (see page 27).

The tetrahedron (**4 faces**) represented the **Fire** element, the cube or hexahedron (**6 faces**) represented the **Earth** element, the octahedron (**8 faces**) represents the **Air** element, the icosahedron (**20 faces**) the

CHAPTER 1

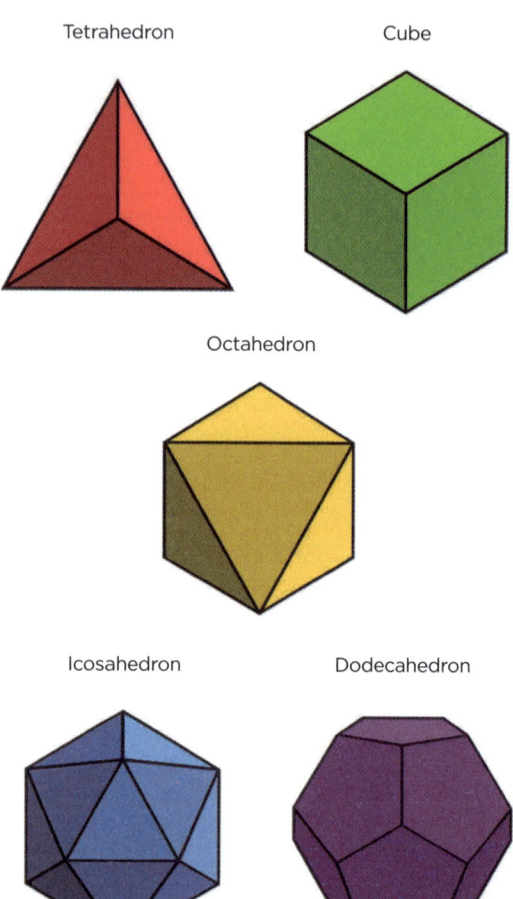

The Platonic Solids

Water element, and the dodecahedron (**12 faces**) represented the **Ether** (or the heavens – Plato assigned the 12 faces to the 12 constellations known at the time).

Together, the Platonic Solids provided ancient Greece with a geometric model of their cosmos (the universe) rooted in numbers. Modern science revealed that these shapes, which represent the basic elements, are the building blocks that make up our world. They appear throughout nature, from crystals and molecular structures to human DNA. What makes the Platonic Solids unique is that every face is a regular polygon of the same size and shape. There are no other possibilities for a closed convex solid to be formed. For example, four squares or three hexagons at each corner would result in a flat surface, similar to floor tiles. Thus, Platonic Solids enjoy special attributes, or characteristics:

✳ All the faces are regular and congruent.

✳ Platonic Solids are convex polyhedrons.

✳ The faces of a Platonic Solid only intersect at their edges.

✳ At each vertex, the same number of faces meet.

✳ Polygonal faces of Platonic Solids share comparable form, height, angles, and edges.

CHAPTER 1

To put it simply, the link between numbers and geometric forms began with a dot and a circle, with the dot representing matter and the circle representing the environment, or space around that matter. When two circles overlap, a line can be drawn across the centre of the sector they produce. Drawing two more lines towards the sector's tip formed a triangle. As the process was replicated, new geometric forms emerged. The Pythagorean philosophers who followed discovered a link between geometric forms and numbers. They developed the Platonic Solids and gave mystical attributes to them in an effort to understand the interconnections within our universe.

For example, the number **4** was regarded to be the perfect number to represent the four elements, the four seasons and the four phases of the moon. It is also the most stable shape (the square) which can be built on. It is the tetrad (see page 36), which signified justice and the ultimate truth of what is physically manifest. In addition, the most ideal number was **ten**, because it is the number from which all other numbers arose.

By the 18th century, Western esotericists expanded on Pythagorean knowledge and ideologies, and it became known as Sacred Geometry (however, these amazing shapes are being discovered all across the world and are thousands of years older than Plato). Furthermore, they embedded much of the meaning of numerology as cycles of personal development and evolution of the soul by adding numbers to images. The latter became known as the Tarot cards – more about that in the next chapter, where we unlock the mystical vibrational meaning of numbers.

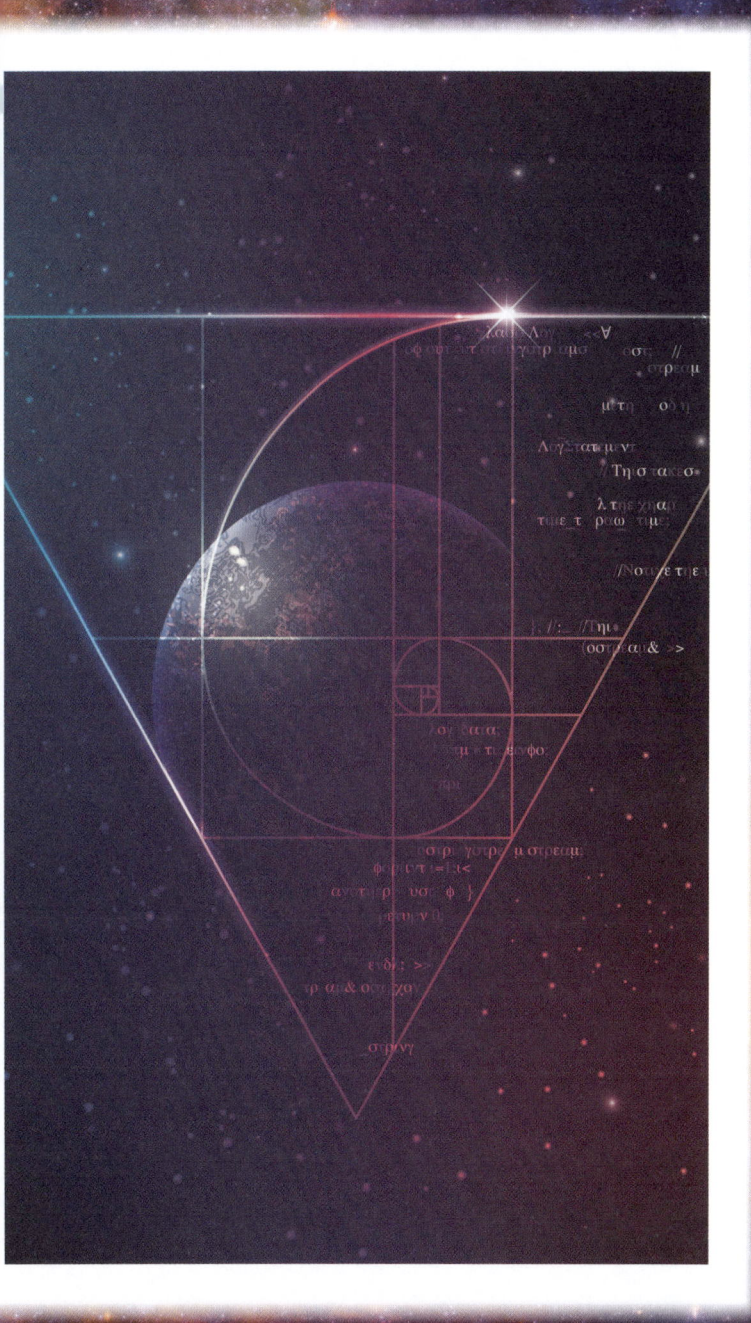

CHAPTER 1

Early philosophers discovered harmony in numbers. The symbolism and beauty of each number can be extended to encompass the essence of all subsequent numbers. The enigmatic nature of Pythagoras and his followers' theories is undeniably motivating and symbolic. Numbers were thought of as geometric shapes that allowed calculations, where geometry was a way of understanding and expressing the universe in equations and numbers. Moreover, the earliest text that mentions how the ancient Greeks saw the universe in numbers is *Lives of the Philosophers, Successions of the Philosophers* (circa 1st century BCE), which quotes from a text called *Pythagorean Memoirs*:

'The principle of all things is a monad [see page 34]. *And from the monad the indefinite dyad exists, like matter for the monad, its cause. From the monad and the indefinite dyad come the numbers, and from the numbers the points. From them come lines, out of which come planar figures. From planes come solid figures, and from these, sense-perceptible bodies, from which come the four elements—Fire, Water, Earth, Air.'*

The circle is the parent shape of all the shapes that follow it. When a circle is mirrored, it produces two circles. These two circles placed side by side (see page 22) form the foundation for all numbers:

Number 1 – Monad: Unity

Number 1 is represented by a circle with a dot at the centre (see below), known as the monad. Ancient mathematical philosophers started with a point and drew a circle around it, believing that nothing exists without a centre. In regard to other numbers, the monad preserves the identity of everything it encounters. Any number multiplied by one equals itself, as does any number divided by one. It therefore symbolized number 1, The Essence of The Unity, or the Foundation. In order for 'one to become many', the circle (or one) must be transformed by a reflection.

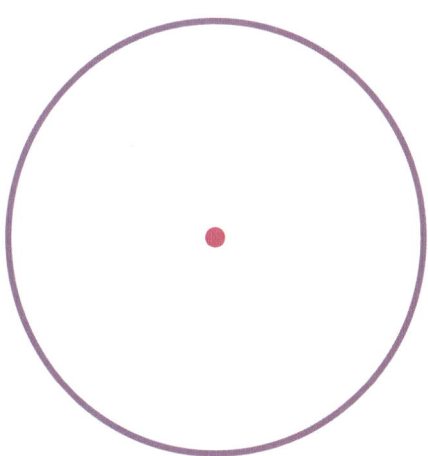

Number 1 – Monad

CHAPTER 1

Number 2 – Dyad: Power Limited/unlimited

The dyad was dubbed 'audacity' by Greek philosophers because of the boldness of separation from the one, and 'anguish' because there is still a sense of tension from a desire to return to oneness. They believed that the dyad divides and unites, repels and attracts, separates and returns. Number two represents the bridge that connects the One and the Many.

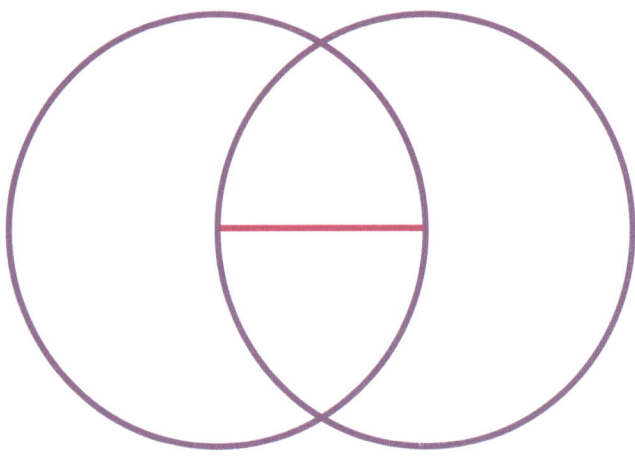

Number 2 – Dyad

THE VIBRATIONS OF NUMBERS

Number 3 – Triad: Harmony

Number three represents the 'first born' out of the union of numbers 1 and 2. The equilateral triangle is its geometric representation. The number 3 is the only number equal to the sum of the previous numbers. For instance, one plus two equals three. Three is also the only number whose sum equals its product: Or 1 + 2 + 3 = 1 x 2 x 3. Number 3 symbolizes prudence, wisdom, piety, friendship, peace and harmony. The triangle represents balance and is a polygon of stability and strength.

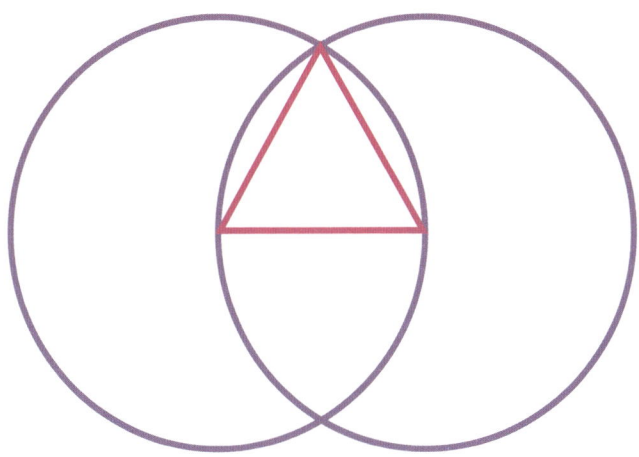

Number 3 – Triad

CHAPTER 1

Number 4 – Tetrad: The Cosmos

Philosophers pondered the creation of the tetrad. It is formed by drawing a horizontal and vertical line linking the centres and intersecting points of the two circles. When a circle is drawn along the line connecting the two centres, a perfect square exists within the circle representing number 4 (see below). Number 4 symbolizes justice, balance, wholeness, and fulfilment. It represents the four seasons and the four directions. Four is the first number created by the addition and multiplication of equals (2 x 2= 4, 2+2 = 4). And because is the first such number, it was thought of as the first 'female' or feminine number.

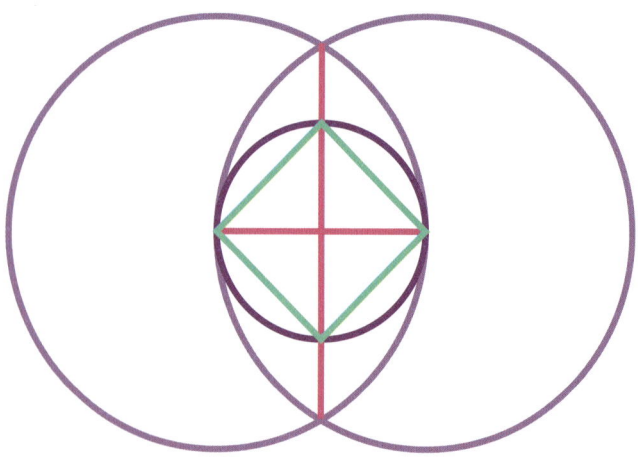

Number 4
– Tetrad (in purple)

Number 5 – Pentad

Number 5 – Pentad: The Five Pointed Star

The fifth geometric figure, or Pentad, denoted the number 5 (see above). It was seen as a sign of life itself. All preceding number symbols are combined to form the pentad: the monad's point, the dyad's line, the triad's surface, and the tetrad's three-dimensional volume. The pentad is also used to refer to the well-known five-point star. The pentad is formed by the existence of the five fingers of the hand, considered an emblem of protection from evil and a symbol of strength and immunity.

Because of the symbol's significance, the formation of the symbol was first kept hidden from society. The pentad was employed by the Pythagoreans as a secret symbol to differentiate themselves and recognise other members. (The five-pointed star,

CHAPTER 1

or pentacle, is one of the four minor suits of the Minor Arcana in the Tarot. In the Major Arcana, it appears as an inverted pentacle on The Devil Card – perhaps as the opposition to life.)

Number 6 – Hexad: Six around One – The Flower of Life

This geometric shape is composed of six identical circles arranged around one circle. Renee Hoadley, an artist who spent years researching and painting numerical sacred geometry and is the founder of Cosmic-core.org, writes 'The seed of life also represents a vortex motion. As the vortex continues to spin and spiral outwards it forms the flower of life, which leads to Metatron's Cube, which contains within it all the Platonic Solids and geometric ratios of music and light.'

Number 6 –Hexad

CHAPTER 1

Number 7 – Heptad: Seven Circles – The Germ of Life

The shape that the seven circles make gives the number 7 its meaning. These seven circles stand in for the diatonic musical scale's seven notes. In modern numerology, 7 is associated with the visible light spectrum of seven colours as well as the seven chakras (or centres of spiritual energy). The seventh circle denotes the last stage of the seven-day 'creation process', which started with a dot and continued through a monad and the physical manifest universe. This symbol is found in various ancient cultures from China to Ancient Egypt, and in medieval churches in Britain. Leonardo da Vinci was aware of the Flower of Life and drew it in his notes. In order to compute angles, proportions, ratios and geometries – many of which he used in his inventions – Da Vinci used the flower of life geometry.

Number 7 – Heptad

Number 8 – Octad

Number 8 – Octad: The Octave

The number 8 stands for the octave. In music, which is where the journey of numbers started, the eighth note is the same as the first, but at a higher octave or higher frequency (vibration). The octave denotes the transition or movement from one level to a higher (or lower) one. The movement can be up (higher) or down (lower).

Number 8 is symbolized by the seed of life growing into the flower of life. It indicates the return of the octave, or the process being repeated but on a higher octave or increased to a higher power.

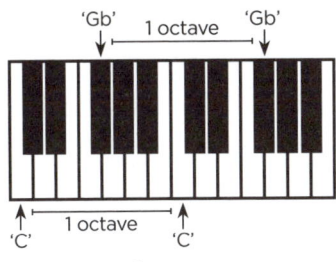

Number 8 – Octave

CHAPTER 1

Number 9 – Nonad: End of A Cycle

In Pythagorean numerology the number 9 symbolizes **the end of one cycle and the beginning of another**. It is represented by the nine-pointed star.

To the Pythagoreans, nine represented the final of the cardinal numbers, or root numbers as they are known in mathematics (end of a cycle). As such, it represents the highest vibrational frequency of any number, excluding the master numbers 11, 22, 33, that we will discuss later.

Number 9 – Nonad

THE VIBRATIONS OF NUMBERS

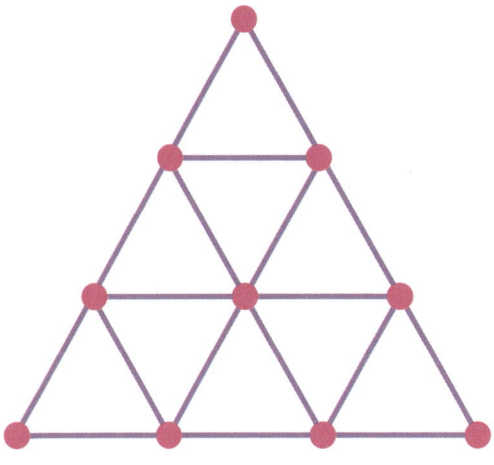

Number 10 – Decad

Number 10 – Decad (or dekad): Unity of the Higher Order

To the Pythagoreans, a single point equals one, a line equals two (since a line has two ends), a triangle equals three, and space equals four. As a result, 10 represented all potential spaces. Pythagoras wrote in his book *Aetius* that the power of the number 10 lies in the number 4, the tetrad: if one starts with the unit (1) and adds the subsequent numbers up to 4, one will get the number 10 (1 + 2 + 3 + 4 = 10). So, number 10 as a unit is number 10, but its potential lies in number 4.

The next figure demonstrates that tetrad of the decad, also known as the tetractys of the decad, representing number 10 as an equilateral triangle, by arranging the first 10 numbers in

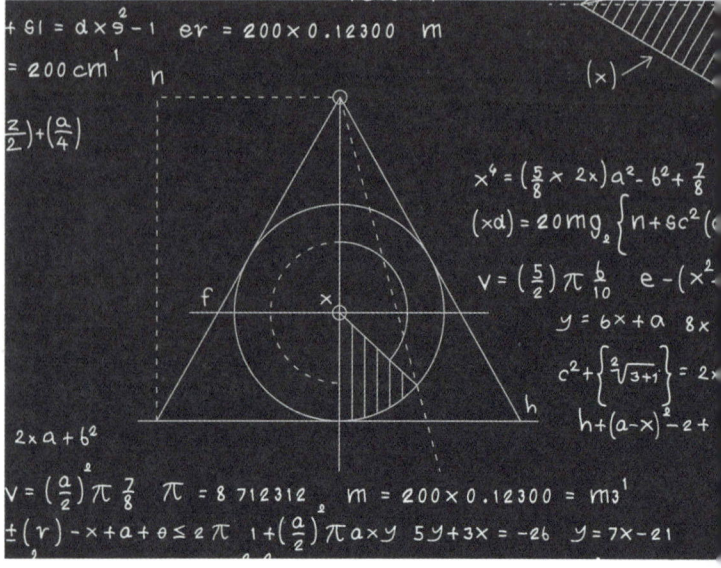

four rows, with 1, 2, 3 and 4 points in each row, respectively. This shape or symbol was a significant mystical emblem in Pythagoreanism's hidden worship, as Priya Hemenway describes in her book *Divine Proportion* (Sterling Publishing, 2006).

Tip: Keep the number 'qualities' above in mind when you come to interpret the vibrational meaning of life-path numbers. A good way to unlock your intuition when interpreting numerology life-path numbers is to ask yourself, 'how can I express the essence, or the characteristics of this number?' Write one word in your numerology journal to describe the essence of each number. Even better, try your hand at drawing a representation of that number that is meaningful to you.

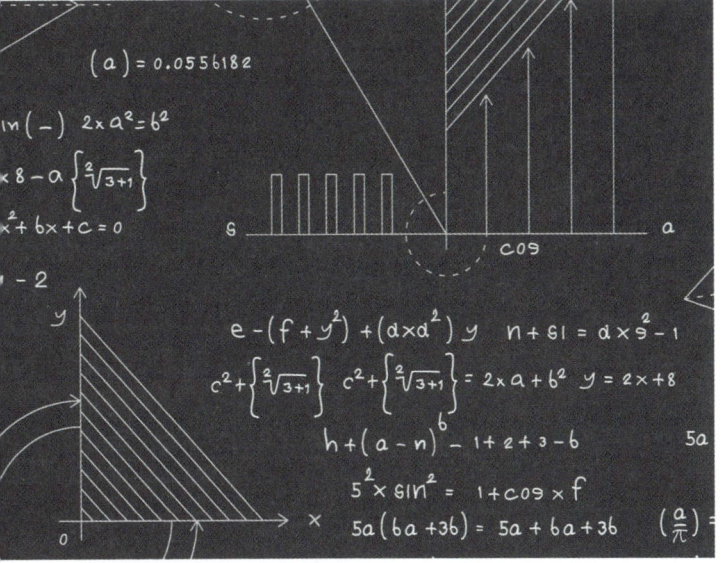

The Significance of Number 10

Number 10 is significant in modern numerology. And although a symbol representing zero first appeared in the Babylonian system during the 3rd century BCE, zero as a number was not used consistently in mathematical calculations. Zero seemed to mark inner locations. The difference between 77 and 7,700 was impossible to identify unless by context. The use of decimals and zero as a number appeared around the 8th century as a result of the 9th-century, Persian polymath Al-Khwarizmi's work.

To the Pythagoreans number **10** was considered a sacred number owing to the fact that it is the sum of the first four digits (1+2+3+4=10) and is the basis of forming geometric shapes (see page 26). Number 10 was also thought of as the most perfect

number, because all numbers arise from it. In other words, it represented unity arising from multiplicity. Moreover, the sacredness of the number ten inspired a list of ten essential polar opposites, as Dudley mentioned in his book:

- Limited and unlimited
- Odd and even
- One and many
- Right and left
- Masculine and feminine
- Rest and motion
- Straight and crooked
- Light and darkness
- Good and evil
- Square and oblong

If you will, the zero adds potential to any number's vibration. Although in numerology numbers are reduced to one digit (10= 1+ 0), the zero amplifies the potential expressed by any number that has a zero in it before it is reduced to one digit. Keep that in mind when you practise name or birthdate numerology.

CHAPTER 1

Pythagorean Master Numbers

Numbers 11, 22, and 33, known as **Master Numbers**, were not reduced to a single number because they form The Triangle of Enlightenment (see below). Number **11** represented the feminine (1+1=2), **22** represented the masculine (2+2=4); together they form the foundation, or the perfect harmony to grow and evolve to.

The highest point of evolution Perfect Harmony was represented by the apex of the triangle, denoting that the collaboration of both aspects, feminine and masculine, leads to perfect harmony or union represented by number 33 (3+3=6).

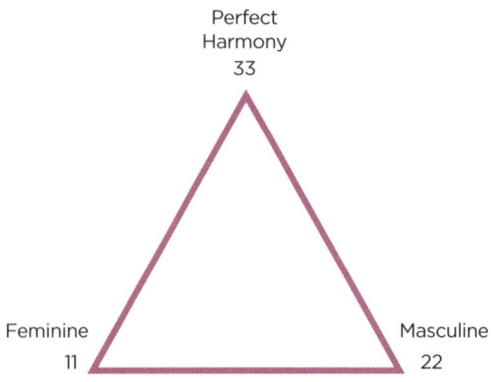

The Triangle of Enlightenment, Master Numbers

Number six in the Tarot, for instance, is represented by The Lovers Card, where you see a man and woman standing under an angel (harmony) with a mountain, their goal, behind them (triangle). We will look at Tarot numerology in Chapter Two.

Moreover, other double digits are considered **Power Numbers** since the same number is reinforcing its vibration by doubling and hence has strong vibrations. However, although the energy of power numbers is strongly felt, they are not as intense as Master Numbers.

The following table, on page 40, offers a summary of Pythagorean geometry of numbers, where through movement, or vibration, more numbers were 'created'.

CHAPTER 1

LIFE-PATH NUMBER	KEYWORD	INTERPRETATION
1	Unity/Potential	Essence, Foundation, multiplied by its reflection.
2	Power/Duality	Dual power that separates and unites. The Bridge: the bridge that connects one to many.
3	Harmony	Harmony achieved by balanced duality. Expansion: through Union, the fist born is created.
4	Cosmos	The Foundation from which anything can become manifest.
5	Five-Pointed Star	Life manifest. Protection. Cycle mid-point.
6	Flower of Life	The basis of forming more shapes.
7	Germ of Life	A pivotal point in the process leading up to the octave.
8	The Octave	Increased, higher power.
9	Cycle End	End of one cycle and the beginning of another.
10	Perfect Number	Heightened potential (Unity arises multiplicity)
11	Master Number	Feminine on A Higher Level, The Visionary
22	Master Number	Masculine on A Higher Level, Master Architect, Builder
33	Master Number	Union On A Higher level Leads to Perfect Harmony

The Pythagorean geometry of numbers

To assist in connecting with the vibrational meaning of your life-path number, use the area below to make a note of it (adding all digits of your birthdate), describing any insights your number evokes so far.

	DD	MM	YYYY
DATE OF BIRTH	__+__	__+__	__+__+__+__
Sub Total	_____	_____	_____
Total reduced to one digit (or a master number reduced to one digit)	__	__	__
Your Life-Path Number			
Your Insights			

CHAPTER 1

Pythagorean Name Numerology

The method of converting words to numbers is crucial to numerology. The practice has its origins in Greek, Latin, and Hebrew *gematria*, or the practice of converting words into numbers for the purpose of divination. People have utilized gematria to study and interpret the Torah, the Bible, and other holy books. Most numerologists concentrate on people's names, employing a simple method to convert names into numbers. Different numerology systems employ different charts, but a simple one begins with A equalling 1, B equalling 2, and so on. Although numerology of names is significant, bear in mind that when it comes to interpretation, it largely depends on the chosen spelling of the name.

1	2	3	4	5	6	7	8	9
A	B	C	D	E	F	G	H	I
J	K	L	M	N	O	P	Q	R
S	T	U	V	W	X	Y	Z	

The alphanumeric chart

Pythagoreans who followed applied numbers to correlate a person's name and date of birth to describe a person's outer character or disposition. Pythagoras spent time in the Near East studying other number systems that were popular at the time, such as the Chaldean number system (used from 625 to 539 BCE), which is thought to be more accurate but more complicated; Zoroastrian philosophy; the Abjad system developed by the Arabs by assigning a numerical value to each letter of the alphabet; and the practice in Jewish tradition of

CHAPTER 1

assigning mystical meanings to words based on their numerical value. However, to date, the Pythagorean number system has been the most popular in various cultures which is based on the first **9** cardinal numbers, 1 to 9.

The table on page 42 includes all of the letters in the alphabet, one for each number from 1 to 9. Name numerology provides a clear perspective on a person's soul purpose and how they relate to or express themselves in their environment. In addition, the person's birthdate is important in gaining insights into their skills, talents and attributes. In name numerology, titles such as Sr, Jr, II or III are not considered. You can, however, analyze account names or company names and compare versions to see which one best meets your goals.

Pythagoreans were thinkers, philosophers and mathematicians who attempted to understand a person's life purpose through numbers. Generally, Pythagorean numerology is made up of six different variants and vibrations of numerology:

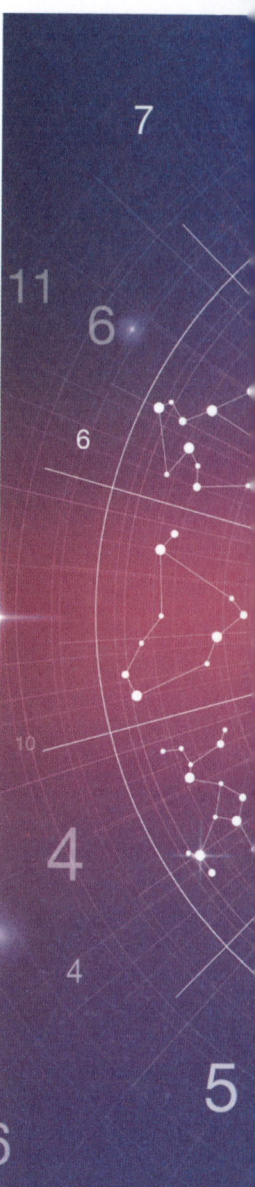

* Life-path number (birth-force number)

* Birth-day number

* First-impression number

* Inner soul number (soul-urge number)

* Character number (personality number)

* Expression number (destiny number)

Life-Path Number

The life-path number is the focus of the Pythagorean numerology system. This is the total of your date of birth reduced to one number, and it represents your life experiences and the lessons you will learn throughout your lifetime. Sometimes this number is also referred to as the birth-force number (Master Numbers are considered before they are reduced to a single digit as they provide additional insights).

Birth-Day Number

Your birth-day number is the number of the day you were born in the month. It vibrates your personality qualities, unique abilities and talents that will help you throughout your life. It is determined by simply your day of your birth, reduced to one digit. So, for example, if you were born on the 12th day of a month, your birth-day number will be 3. 1+2=3.

First-Impression Number

The first-impression number expresses what people think of you when they first meet you. It is calculated by adding only the birth-day and month numbers together.

Soul-Urge Number

In Pythagorean numerology, the soul-urge number is regarded as the third most important number. It is often referred to as the 'inner soul' number. It depicts what your heart truly craves or your soul longs for on a deep level. It generally reveals how the individual is on the inside. It is calculated by adding all of the numbers corresponding to vowels in a person's name (first and last name) and then reducing them to a single digit. Furthermore, the soul-urge number reveals a person's subconscious desire, which is commonly overlooked while living in the physical or material world. This number may have an impact on a person's professional and personal life by attracting careers or persons with whom they connect or resonate.

Character Number

The character number is derived by adding all of the consonants in a person's first and last name. It is also known as the 'personality number,' and it reflects how a person acts and expresses themselves when they meet someone new. In other words, it depicts a person's outer personality. To determine the character number, add the numbers corresponding to all of the consonants in the name, both first and last name, then reduce the total to a single digit.

The Expression Number

The expression number is also referred to as the destiny number. To determine the destiny number, add together all the numbers that correspond to the entire

THE VIBRATIONS OF NUMBERS

birth name. Destiny numbers represent a person's strengths and weaknesses that they have developed from birth. Furthermore, it expresses any latent qualities or talents they possess, as well as the challenges they must overcome throughout their lifetime. It may also reveal what skills might be learned that could be useful in assisting a person attaining their life goals.

CHAPTER 2
Numerological Interpretations

CHAPTER 2

Pythagorean philosophy and numerology influenced the Muslim scholars of the 12th century, who translated their works. The latter built on the knowledge they had from Eastern and Indian schools of thought. Their translated works, as well their own contributions, influenced modern-day mainstream science. By the 18th century, Platonic concepts also became the foundation of 'hidden knowledge' that influenced the Enlightenment movement.

Sacred, or secret, knowledge of the interrelationship of all things in our universe had to be 'preserved' since the church banned such 'unorthodox' ideas in the Middle Ages. By the 18th century, Western esotericists developed the Pythagorean concepts of elements, numbers, alphabets and geometric shapes, and it became known as Sacred Geometry.

Knowledge that was considered sacred or 'spiritual' was coded and then reflected in a variety of disciplines – for instance, the Tarot. There's no doubt that the Rider-Waite-Smith Tarot deck exhibited this. The latter was the first English-language fully illustrated Tarot deck with instructions. It contained plenty of symbolism 'encoded' in its drawings. These methods of encoding or conserving old information included the Kabbalah and other fields that are now familiar to us, like astrology.

It was in the 18th century that illustrated Tarot cards were assigned numbers to convey their numerical vibrational qualities, symbolizing the cycles of personal development and spiritual enlightenment. The Tarot is comprised of 22 Major cards (major cycles) and 56 Minor cards (minor cycles) classified

NUMEROLOGICAL INTERPRETATIONS

into the four Platonic elements of nature. The vibrational meaning of each number is attributed to pictures in the major as well as minor cards. The ascending numbers and their images also denote developmental personal-growth cycles – the trials and tribulations that a person, represented by The Fool, goes through to self-transform and fulfil their destiny.

CHAPTER 2

Major Cycles

In the Tarot, the journey of self-development starts with The Fool. Growth is a journey, and the cards were numbered to reflect that journey and the cycles of change and transformation. **The Fool** card represents each of us at the beginning of our self-discovery journey. It symbolizes the unlimited potential within each of us. Next, is number **1** which was ascribed to **The Magician**, who is depicted standing in front of nature's four elements and seasons, or cycles of change. Number 1 denotes the initiation of ideas into action and contains all possibilities or processes (and numbers) to materializing whatever we desire.

Moreover, in the Minor cards of the Tarot, we meet the four seasons again. Each has its own series of cards, numbered form 1 to 10, denoting minor cycles of change within each seasonal process of growth (more details on page 58).

NUMEROLOGICAL INTERPRETATIONS

CHAPTER 2

NUMEROLOGICAL INTERPRETATIONS

To the Pythagoreans, the following number, **2**, represented duality and was thought of as **feminine.** In the Tarot, it is assigned to **The High Priestess**, while number **3** was thought of as **masculine** (assigned to **The Empress,** the counterpart of **The Emperor**). **The Emperor** card depicted authority, self-mastery of the dual aspect of logic and intuition, which leads to stability, symbolizing the earth element, the vibration of stability. Geometrically, the number 4 is expressed as a square, which is the most stable geometric shape. The Emperor also came to represent the 'builder', who creates from the four elements of nature, and manifests results in the physical world.

And since the sum of two and three is five, the number **5** represented marriage, the coming together of the feminine and the masculine; it was assigned to **The Hierophant**, or the high priest, denoting matrimonial prospects and spiritual marriage in a church.

Tip: If you are familiar with the Tarot, you might recall spotting images of geometric shapes: triangle, square, pyramid or a circle and stars. Often these shapes are 'hidden' within the image of the card and carry additional information.

The table on page 58 summarizes the process of The Fool's growth and the interpretation of the numbers assigned to this journey.

CHAPTER 2

The numbering of the cards (see page 56) refers to the original numbers assigned to the cards in the Tarot of Marseille, where Justice was number 8, as the expression of balance, rather than the much later Rider-Waite-Smith deck, which was based on astrological correspondences worked out by the Hermetic Order of the Golden Dawn.

LIFE-PATH NUMBER	KEYWORD	MAJOR TAROT CARD
1	Inner resources, initiative	THE MAGICIAN
2	Heightened sensitivity	THE HIGH PRIESTESS
3	Expansion, joy, creativity	THE EMPRESS
4	Stability, structure, attainment	THE EMPEROR
5	Freedom, heightened awareness	THE HIEROPHANT
6	Harmony	THE LOVERS
7	Self-mastery, perseverance	THE CHARIOT
8	Delicate balance, karma	JUSTICE (card 11 in some decks)
9	Fulfilment	THE HERMIT

Keyword Tarot numerology of Major cards

NUMEROLOGICAL INTERPRETATIONS

Minor Cycles

The Tarot's Minor Arcana, which resembles a deck of paying cards we are all familiar with, is comprised of four suits. Each suit has 10 numbered images in ascending order from 1 to 10 (known as pip cards), and four royal cards (known as the Court Cards). The latter are Pages, Knights, Queens and Kings, where the King and Queen represent the culmination of the developmental cycle of each Page, having attained sovereignty or self-mastery as King or Queen.

Furthermore, each of the four suits of the pip cards represent daily life situations; the **Wands** (clubs) denote the spring season, symbolizing initiating action, when seeds are planted in the earth. Next is summer, denoted by the **Cups** (hearts) suit, symbolizing watering the seed and nurturing it (emotions); this is followed by the **Swords** (spades), the autumn season, when crops are harvested, symbolizing mental activity and thoughts; and finally the **Pentacles** (diamonds) represent worldly achievements, symbolized by the coin or pentacle, denoting material gain form selling the crops. The completion of each cycle leads to further transformation. In some ways, personal development is never-ending. It is similar to ascending numbers, where adding a digit to a number results in the creation of a new number, or further development. The Minor cards represent seasonal as well as personal cycles of change. The four suits represent the four developmental processes one must pass through in order to acquire the knowledge and experiences required to go on to the next number and achieve self-mastery. Namely, these developmental cycles are putting ideas or thoughts into action (Wands), managing emotions (Cups), mastering the mind (Swords), which leads to the 'manifest' result of material gain respectively (Pentacles).

A brief description of the minor cycles of self-development as represented by the Minor cards numbered 1 to 10 is as follows.

1 – Growth
Number 1 is the cycle's commencement, or the possibility of what might develop or grow. It denotes the beginning of what will emerge or take place by the growth cycle's conclusion. It suggests the start of a process or the beginning of an action.

2 – Harmony
Two represents the start of progress, which entails separation or balanced duality. Number 2 suggests the existence of two opposing forces that must be balanced (logic and intuition).

3 – Expansion
Three depicts the outcome of the merger of two forces, or the result of collaboration. It might be the start of something bigger, such as expansion, or tension as the two interact.

NUMEROLOGICAL INTERPRETATIONS

CHAPTER 2

4 – Stability
Stability is achieved at this stage of development. Four provides the groundwork for future growth, development or progress. Further development can be made if the foundation is strong and one is devoted to the 'process' or journey. Commitment to achieving goals is required, as well as discipline and methodology.

5 – Adjustments
The fifth number represents the cycle's midpoint. Just because a firm foundation was laid, it does not mean that one can relax their dedication or commitment. Progress is a process that can bring changes at any time. Unforeseen changes may throw one

off at any time if balance is not maintained. Number 5 might signify change, new opportunities or unforeseen conflict in which the terms of involvement must be renegotiated (of the initial union of two).

6 – Flow
Once 'negotiations' are complete and adjustments are made, the vibration of number 6 signifies a phase of ease and flow.

7 – Perseverance
The number 7 symbolizes the choice between giving up and enduring at pivotal point in one's life journey. It indicates a struggle in which extra effort is required to overcome any

roadblocks that may develop. If difficulties are to be overcome, self-mastery of one's intellect and emotions is required. Nothing must be taken for granted. Caution and deliberate action are required.

8 – Development

Moving forward or letting go. As one's life journey unfolds, transformation is necessary to prepare for the final phases of development. Number 8 resembles a delicate balance; any wrong or right decision or action can have immediate profound effects. In a way, it is seen as a karmic number, where cause and effect play out almost immediately.

9 – Reflection

Number 9 is the cycle's last phase, where rest can be enjoyed after some reflection on the results obtained thus far. The current cycle's outcome may be fruitful. If, on the other hand, it is not, it is time to reassess and accept any limitations. One can prepare for the next growth cycle by remaining flexible.

10 – Renewal

Number 10 contains the commencement stage as well as the untapped potential. It increases the potential and contains all of the elements necessary for expression or manifestation in the physical world. Because growth is ongoing, it marks the start of a new cycle on a higher octave, as well as a moment for renewal before continued progress.

CHAPTER 2

Number 1

Life cycle

The start of a new cycle of growth. It relates to uncovering what we are capable of and learning how to realize our dreams. It is about consciousness expressing its fullest potential. This life cycle teaches us to trust our inner abilities and own who we are, achieving tangible results in the physical world. It is about individuation, self-empowerment, and recognizing our unique expression (whatever that may be). This is the first step to manifesting 'divine inspiration'; action (movement) is required. Through action, the soul discovers what it can achieve and how to express its individuality as it communicates with others and learns that we are equally unique.

Keywords

Action. Movement. Travel.

The initiator, the leader, the 'Jack and master of all trades' is number 1. The task of number 1 is to put ideas into action in order to achieve success and fulfil their purpose. They have both an organized and intuitive mind. In order to lead well, the leader's mind has to

NUMEROLOGICAL INTERPRETATIONS

be a flexible one, and balanced between methodology, creativity and logic. In this way, their actions are appropriate and timely. Number 1 inspires their team members to develop their fullest potential too, offering support, knowledge and expertise.

Although number 1 is content to work alone, they frequently need to collaborate with others to see their ideas through to completion. Communication is a key word for number 1. Ideas must be expressed clearly and eloquently, which makes them superb keynote speakers, writers, journalists or marketing and social media professionals. Moreover, they appreciate the beauty of simplicity, which makes them articulate mentors, editors or designers.

Their life-path challenge is to learn how to materialize their ideas using the gifts they were born with. They are inquisitive, and are interested in the creative arts, languages, travel, culture, as well as the methodology or procedure by which things work. 'How can I make this happen?' is what they are thinking. As a result, they make exceptional designers, multimedia artists, engineers, writers and architects as well as coaches and counsellors. Number 1 is all about figuring out how to do it and then executing it, which contributes to their success as entrepreneurs.

CHAPTER 2

Number 2

Life cycle
Honing intuition. Now that belief in one's unique purpose and abilities is established – as is the knowledge that acquiring skills is essential to manifesting any potential – the soul learns about its dual nature. As it acts in the material world it must also perceive (inspiration). Perception of the unknown happens through the inner senses of a person. Intuition helps the soul maintain balanced earthly existence while 'listening' to higher guidance.

Keywords
Mindful awareness. Surrender to the unknown. Collaboration.

They may be unclear about their passion or vocation in life, but they are always nurturing, kind people who 'feel' their way through life. Number 2 people have strong intuition or psychic potential. They may be reserved in expressing their emotions and say very little, but they are very perceptive of other vibrations, and people and their moods. This quality can make them a sponge for the emotions of others.

NUMEROLOGICAL INTERPRETATIONS

Number 2 people recognize the subtleties of things in life. They are sensitive to sound, music, singing, poetry, the rhythm of lunar cycles and the passage of day and night throughout the year. When grounded, they are almost always in touch with their inner intuition or guidance, which can make them outstanding healers, psychics, mediums, singers or musicians.

Number 2 is a highly imaginative number, where overthinking might stymie their progress and lead them nowhere fast. As a result, their task is to stay in the now and master their thoughts so that their mind works for them rather than against them. Often, a step becomes clear only after the previous one is taken. The second task is to trust, surrender and let go. They can handle any position in a professional career due to their strong intuition, as long as they remain flexible, observe their surroundings and avoid becoming caught in their own thoughts.

If you draw cards 20, 29 or 38, these are all connected to the number 2 in different, less direct, vibrations. The number 38 reaches 2 via the Master Number 11 and so is doubly linked to the feminine and the qualities outlined above.

CHAPTER 2

Number 3

Life Cycle
Fruition. This is the number of bringing things into being. It is the first born out of the union of numbers 1 and 2, and so has all the qualities of expansion and fecundity.

Keywords
Abundance. Expansion. Harmony.

Number 3 is the 'trinity' of numbers. It blends ingenuity, beauty and abundance. Number 3 people can 'give birth' to any creative or business enterprise in any endeavour. They have a loving, caring and nurturing temperament and appreciate the

beauty of all things in life. They value nature, being outdoors, gardening, flowers, colours, the companionship of family and friends, and meeting people from diverse cultures. They can be successful in any field, but especially in communications, media, publishing, running a home-grown business or managing an art gallery.

Within its consciousness, number 3 has the ability to understand the abstract as well as the logical. They

NUMEROLOGICAL INTERPRETATIONS

perceive the vibrations of sound, visual images or colour, and can understand abstract thoughts, innovative ideas and concepts such as sacred geometry, patterns, or 'codes' to unlock life's mysteries. They are practical thinkers who enjoy the fruits of their labour and all that life has to offer. Others are uplifted by their optimism and they can inspire themselves and others to great feats. They are also great peace-makers who would do well in diplomatic professions such as arbitration or indeed governmental diplomacy.

Drawing this card can also indicate an actual pregnancy. This is also the case for the card 39, which has both 3 and 9, the numbers of creation and the end of a cycle, on it and so contains the vibration of physical birth. Cards 12, 21 and 30 have less direct number 3 energy, but nevertheless they contain the same qualities. With cards 12 and 21, you are able to meditate on the union of 1 and 2 in two different ways – with 1 leading 2 and then with 2 leading 1.

CHAPTER 2

Number 4

Life Cycle
Stability. This is the number of creating everlasting impact through consistent effort. It is the building blocks with which anything can become manifest.

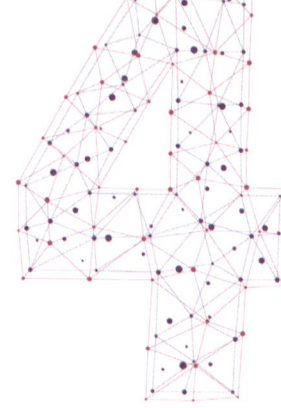

Keywords
Structure. Process. Foundation.

The vibration of number 4 is all about structure and methodology. They have a fair, practical and grounded approach to realizing their life goals, ideas, projects or any other undertaking. Although they are diligent 'builders' who demand our respect, generally they are not innovative and can be resistant to accepting other people's progressive contributions. As community or task leaders, they value facts. They are fair when settling disputes or making decisions.

NUMEROLOGICAL INTERPRETATIONS

Their head is never in the clouds. They work deliberately towards achieving their goals and aspirations. The projects, companies or structures they 'build' have an everlasting impact on their community or in their field. Number 4 people care for all whom they work with or oversee in their community. Generally, they are an intelligent authority figure, with few words, but being quietly helpful to those who need their advice.

Number 4 vibrates rational 'conservative leadership'. People who are influenced by the number 4, or who have the number 4 prominent in their numerology chart, excel in architecture, government, civil service or the law. Their life path may lead them to become good judges, CEOs, community leaders or advocates. Their challenge is to avoid becoming authoritarian or inflexible in their outlook on life (or in any field).

This rigidity can be softened in cards 13 and 31, since both contain numbers 1 and 3. However, remember that number 3 in Tarot numerology is considered a masculine number so those 'left brain' qualities are still here. The card for number 40 is a less direct manifestation of 4.

CHAPTER 2

Number 5

Mid Life- cycle
Adapting to change, liberation and building resilience are the main factors at this stage in the cycle.

Keywords
Flexibility. Protection. Celebration.

The fifth vibration is the 'life and soul' of life's celebration – a breath of fresh air, if you will. With number 5, anything is possible since it promises unexpected opportunities, change and freedom. Like mercury, they are quick to adapt, understand others, and act in any circumstance, environment or culture.

They can effortlessly communicate with people of any age or culture, including youngsters. Their impact and influence is subtle – however, it is always present.

Sometimes number 5 is referred to as 'the oracle' because they have an all-knowing mind and can readily access their inner counsel when questioned about any dilemma or issue. They are mostly unaware of this spiritual connection and present a quiet, serene demeanour. People carrying

NUMEROLOGICAL INTERPRETATIONS

the number 5 excel in the performing arts (they are able to get into character easily and express it fully).

Their challenge is to 'stick to the plan'. They are often simultaneously attracted to several endeavours or fields in which they can easily excel. However, they get distracted from their initial goal just as easily, and never finish what they started. Their task is to commit! Because they value freedom of expression and live their own way, they can overindulge and be reckless.

When the cards 14 and 41 are drawn, this lends some stability to the number 5 energy, ensuring that there is some vibrational help in sticking to a goal or activity. This is due to the presence of the number 4.

Likewise, 23 and 32 channel the energy of the numbers 2 and 3, bringing an extra element of emotional intelligence to the number 5. If you draw one of these cards when wanting information on romantic relationships, this is a good sign and should encourage you to move forward knowing there is a bit of good vibrational energy here for a union.

CHAPTER 2

Number 6

Life Cycle
Knowing oneself through partnering with others. This is the vibration of creating harmonious partnerships and materializing goals by collaborating with others. It is about coming together with others who share similar tasks and learning to cooperate.

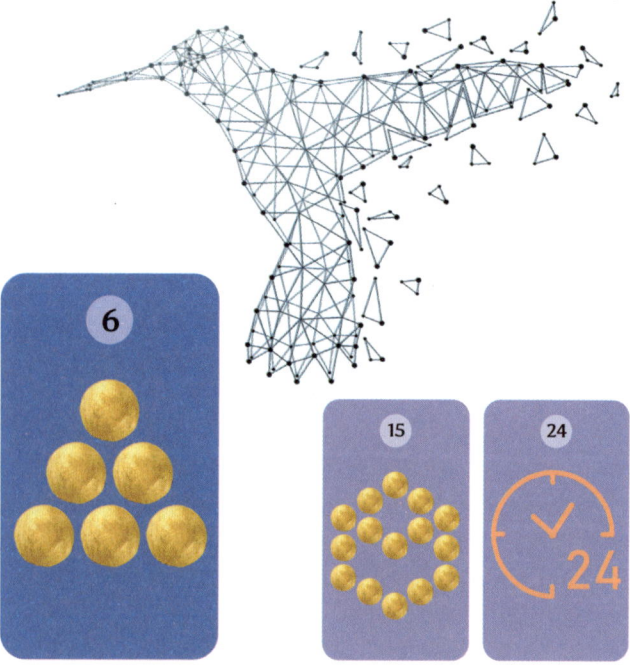

NUMEROLOGICAL INTERPRETATIONS

Keywords

Transformation. Decisions. Balance. Service to others.

One of the first choices we make as individuals looking for our own distinctive expression in life is who we will share our lives with or cooperate with to achieve further goals. These common goals can be creating a business partnership, starting a family or sharing a joyful life together.

Furthermore, number 6 is a transformational vibration. It encourages people to get to know themselves better through engaging with others. We are often drawn to collaborating with others who 'mirror' aspects of ourselves in some way. These aspects are usually a mix of positive and negative. The task of number 6 is to identify these aspects, find balance and grow further. On a wider scale, number 6 can be drawn to connect with a group of people to achieve common goals, or serve higher goals for community, society and all living creatures.

Despite being uniquely different from their partners, the task of number 6 is to make decisions that lead to harmony and balance. Maintaining this balance produces emotional stability, which inspires number 6 to pursue and achieve further new and impactful goals.

The impact of cards 15 and 24 are more dependent on their component numbers than the more direct card 6. So 15 is comprised of the creation energy of 1 and the celebration energy of 5. Card 24 has the union of 2 and the stability of 4. Each of these subset cards highlight the energy of that relationship.

CHAPTER 2

Number 7

Life cycle
Mastery of senses, urges, emotions and mind. This number bridges spiritual and earthly natures. It represents victory over all obstacles.

Keywords
Transcendence. Victory. Pivotal point.

Having learned how to establish balance in partnerships, number 7 is propelled to undergo further development or transformation through the vibration of 7. Number 7 people are often unaware of the masterful equilibrium they can attain;

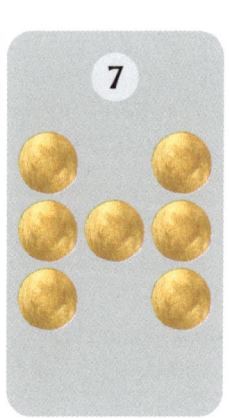

their dual nature as a 'mind in a body' provides them with infinite power and renewable resolve to achieve profound success in material life. When they are awakened to their own nature, they work for divine intelligence. Their own guidance helps them to overcome, and transcend, all kinds of earthly obstacles and score great victories.

As a result, those born under the number 7 have a high potential for 'channelling' or telepathy; they are

NUMEROLOGICAL INTERPRETATIONS

strategic thinkers and planners. They have a unique intellect and are inspired with problem-solving techniques. However, they must work diligently, putting forth consistent effort, and not be distracted by earthly wants or urges.

To achieve success in a cycle of 7, or when a person's life path is 7, they are urged to connect with their spiritual nature on a daily basis, seek a greater purpose for earthly pursuits, and master their instincts in order to overcome hurdles and achieve goals. Their self-awareness will enable them to get unstuck and recover from any down trends quickly. The downside of lack of self-mastery is that it may lead the person to be over-indulgent, or experience fluctuating periods of success and loss. This is due to misguided efforts and can be avoided with self-knowledge and restraint.

Cards 16, 25 and 34 also represent the energy of 7 because the numbers add up to 7. However, how that energy is expressed is also reliant on their component numbers, so also meditate on what the energy of those numbers is when interpreting what a card's appearance indicates.

CHAPTER 2

Number 8

Life cycle
Purification. This is the number of cause-and-effect in the cycle. It can represent profound gains or losses.

Keywords
Higher power. Increase. Balance through heart-centred action.

After achieving balance of emotions, self-mastery of mind and desires, and implementing inspirational direction to gain material victory, the final step before the end of the cycle is about purification and preparing for the end of the process.

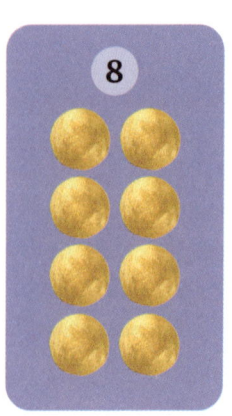

Number 8 resembles the scales of justice or balance. Losses and gains, or cause and effect, play out dramatically and immediately, which why this vibration is sometimes referred to as 'karmic'. The reference here is to the consequences of decisions we make throughout the cycle, according to our intentions or awareness. In a way, this stage of the cycle reflects cumulative self-awareness and growth. This is a stage of 'purification', letting go of the

NUMEROLOGICAL INTERPRETATIONS

past and clearing the way for the new and the grandiose. On a mundane level, this is a cycle of accomplishments on a grand scale. If the person has been committed and sustained their momentum, then this can be the cycle of the fruition of all their invested efforts.

Number 8 signifies material wealth, fame, signing of agreements or significant contracts, and partnerships. On a spiritual level, it augurs the end of a turbulent cycle where one has 'paid' their dues and is about to start a new phase of higher understanding and awareness.

The secondary cards of 17, 26 and 35 embody the energies of the numbers that make them up, as well as the energy of 8 at a lower level. While all iterations of this number are positive, drawing one of the subset cards can indicate that matters are not yet ready to manifest. It may be a nice indication that things are moving in the right direction, but that you may have to wait a little longer before you see the fruits of your labour.

CHAPTER 2

Number 9

Life cycle
Completion. The end of one cycle and the beginning of the next. It represents impacting the collective and giving back.

Keywords
Wisdom. The teacher. Giving.

The vibration of number 9 is that of seeing things through to the end, having earned skills and significant experiences via opportunities and losses. It is through learning to overcome changes, obstacles and differences that you gain self-awareness and wisdom. Then you can pass on that wisdom to others.

The final step, therefore, calls for 'solitude' or withdrawal to reflect on, and assess, the journey so far. The desired priorities and goals may have changed and a new course needs to be charted. If lessons from previous numbers have been learnt, then 9 is the reward of fulfilment, wisdom and higher purpose, and the gift of being able to 'heal', impact and influence others by sharing that wisdom. This is the gift of the teacher archetype.

NUMEROLOGICAL INTERPRETATIONS

The number 9 represents the development of expertise and the accomplishment of any pursued goal or endeavour. People with the number 9 are exceptionally intelligent and wise, and prefer to work alone. They do, however, have a wealth of information and skill that they are happy to share with others. They make outstanding scholars, writers, historians and mentors. They may treasure their privacy and avoid public recognition, yet they are extremely powerful and well-respected in their field or community. The challenge of number 9 is perseverance and a willingness to guide others for the greater benefit.

The secondary number 9 cards of 18, 27 and 36 embody the energies of the numbers they are made up of. So 18 has creative and growth energy and that is what should be meditated upon. Card 27 is one of union and victory combined to bring wisdom to you. It may represent higher learning with a teacher you admire. The number 36 brings the energy of 3 (abundance and harmony) with the relationship joy of 6. This would be a good card for marriage and partnerships.

CHAPTER 2

Number 10

Life cycle
The start of a new cycle of transformation.

Keywords
Amplification of potential and achievement. Quick changes and adjustments.

Number 10 is significant in modern numerology. It amplifies the meanings of number 1 if number 1 is achieved by adding zero to one. This is due to the influence of the zero. Although a symbol representing zero first appeared in the Babylonian system during the third century BCE, as a

number it was not used consistently in mathematical calculations. In fact, the Babylonians displayed zero as two angled wedges. The Mayans used a character that resembled an eye to denote zero and the ancient Chinese are thought to be the ones who first represented zero as a circle which we now use. The Hindus depicted zero as a dot. The mystery around the zero is what causes it to amplify the number 1 when it is reduced from it.

NUMEROLOGICAL INTERPRETATIONS

The secondary cards for this fascinating card are even more dynamic, despite not being the direct card. This is because of the movement between the numbers of the cards before they resolve into the number 10. Card 19 takes the two cards that begin and end the numerological cycle and combine for the powerful energy of 10. Card 28 has more a more home and stability vibe so is good for the purchase of property or a change that impacts where you live. Card 37 is one where more thought is needed before things are resolved. So you may find that others impact your ideas about how to move forward more than you would like. If you can retain your own sense of what you want to manifest, you will find that you can easily adjust and block out any 'noise' around you.

CHAPTER 2

Master Numbers

Because they are made up of 1, 2 and 3, respectively, the numbers 11, 22 and 33 are considered the only Master Numbers in numerology; they form the Triangle of Enlightenment. These profound energies represent the three stages of creation: envisioning, building and imparting. Number 11 is the creator and visionary, number 22 is the architect who builds the vision, and number 33 is the one who delivers it to the material world.

NUMEROLOGICAL INTERPRETATIONS

We use numbers to find the life-path number, which reflects your strengths, limitations and the true nature of who you are. Numerology is more than just adding up your birthdate. These Master Numbers are merely intended to complement your experiences: they are not intended to forge your course through life. Those numbers might help you understand why you responded the way you did in a certain circumstance, if you're not sure why. As you become older, more mature and more self-aware, Master Numbers tend to come into play. They resemble the fundamental vibration of a number or its secondary effect.

If your birthday numbers add up to 11, 22 or 33, you may have a Master Number as your life-path number. For example, if your birthday is 27th July 1995:

✶ Reduce the birth day to one digit = $2 + 7 = 9$

✶ Reduce the month to one digit: July = 7

✶ Reduce the year to one digit: $1 + 9 + 9 + 5 = 24 = 2 + 4 = 6$

✶ Add up the three components: $9 + 7 + 6 = 22$

CHAPTER 2

Master Number 11

Life cycle
The cycle of transformation, healing and mastery.

Keywords
Divine connections. Higher intuition. Intuitive intelligence.

The first Master Number is 11. It represents your subconscious mind, heightened sensitivity and deep, finely tuned intuition. It contains vibrations from number 2 (1 + 1 = 2). Therefore, it is greatly impacted by the leadership of number 1 and collaboration of number 2, and has the ability to execute any endeavour in the material world. Your greatest asset is intuition. You have

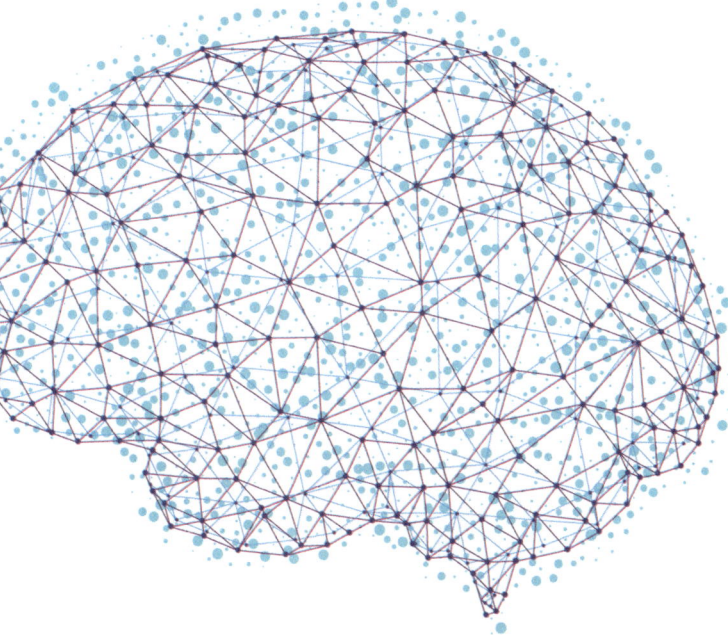

a 'direct' connection to divine intelligence and the cosmos. Logical information may not make sense, so trust your intuition. When not focusing on a particular task or activity, or when overthinking, number 11 can develop severe anxiety. However, they have no trouble generating something extraordinary when they direct all that anxious energy into something tangible.

CHAPTER 2

Master Number 22

Life cycle
This is the cycle of realizing dreams.

Keywords
Master Builder.

The number 22 is also known as the 'Master Builder' or the 'Master Architect'. It contains the number 2, the collaborator, and 4 (2+2), the builder. It is referred to as the most potent of all the others. If worked on with great sincerity, connected with true self and true passions, it has the potential to bring enormous aspirations into fruition. Although those with Master Number life paths have

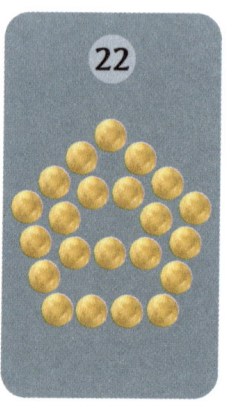

greater potential than others, these potentials must be realized via 'lessons' that must be lived and learned. These folks will experience life's most challenging situations in order to hone their skills, trust their innate abilities and develop self-confidence. They are skilled, disciplined, successful and influential. Resisting Master Number 22 leads to inaction or a complete lack of direction. Number 22 people may realize too late in life that they are unprepared to fulfil their life purpose and accomplishments.

CHAPTER 2

Master Number 33

Life cycle
The cycle of harmony and imparting wisdom.

Keywords
The Master Teacher. Compassion. Profound presence.

Pure love and light are embodied by the number 33. It is referred to as the 'Master Teacher' in numerology because of the immense responsibility of assisting others in finding their path, healing and enlightenment. The universe has trusted them to play this very significant role, and they are fully committed to it.

NUMEROLOGICAL INTERPRETATIONS

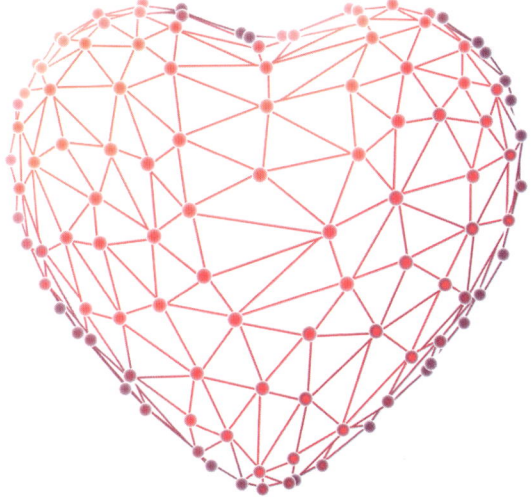

Life path 33 is incredibly rare. Connection to the heart and soul, both of oneself and of others, is its primary vibration. Because they have walked that path themselves, people with this life-path number have been through a lot; they learn (and understand) compassion for others and are able to guide others through their own life journeys. They exhibit grace in the face of adversity and offer others a beacon of hope and healing. The most significant effect of all is made by Master Number 33, which combines the extraordinary capacity for sharing and healing with the manifestation and perceptual powers of the 11 and the 22.

CHAPTER 2

Kabbalah Numerology

Kabbalah numerology has its roots in the Hebrew alphabet and focuses solely on the name given to a person at birth. It is the esoteric interpretation of the 'sacred knowledge' in Jewish mysticism. Moreover, the word 'mysticism' is derived from the Greek verb 'to close' or 'to conceal', dating to Ancient Greece.

The Kabbalah is an old tradition and a complex one; however, the word 'Kabbalah' was previously used in other Judaic contexts, meaning 'received tradition'. It is also the term that mediaeval Kabbalists used to describe their own philosophy in order to convey the idea that they were not inventing anything new, but rather simply disclosing the long-forgotten esoteric tradition of the Torah.

In modern times, 'mysticism' has come to refer to the desire for connection with the Absolute, the Infinite, or God. The intention of Kabbalah numerology is to connect you to your own inner resources, providing insight, meaning and knowledge for self- discovery. In order to gain understanding, the Kabbalah system requires people to be honest with themselves as they reflect on their life path back to the 'source'. This journey, if you like, is expressed by the Kabbalah Tree of Life. It illustrates the spiritual path of ascent by man, who is seen as a microcosm of divine creation, and serves as a symbol of God's nature and his relationship to the created universe. The 22 numbered lines, or vibrations, indicate the main mystical paths, or requirements, to be acquired between the spheres in order

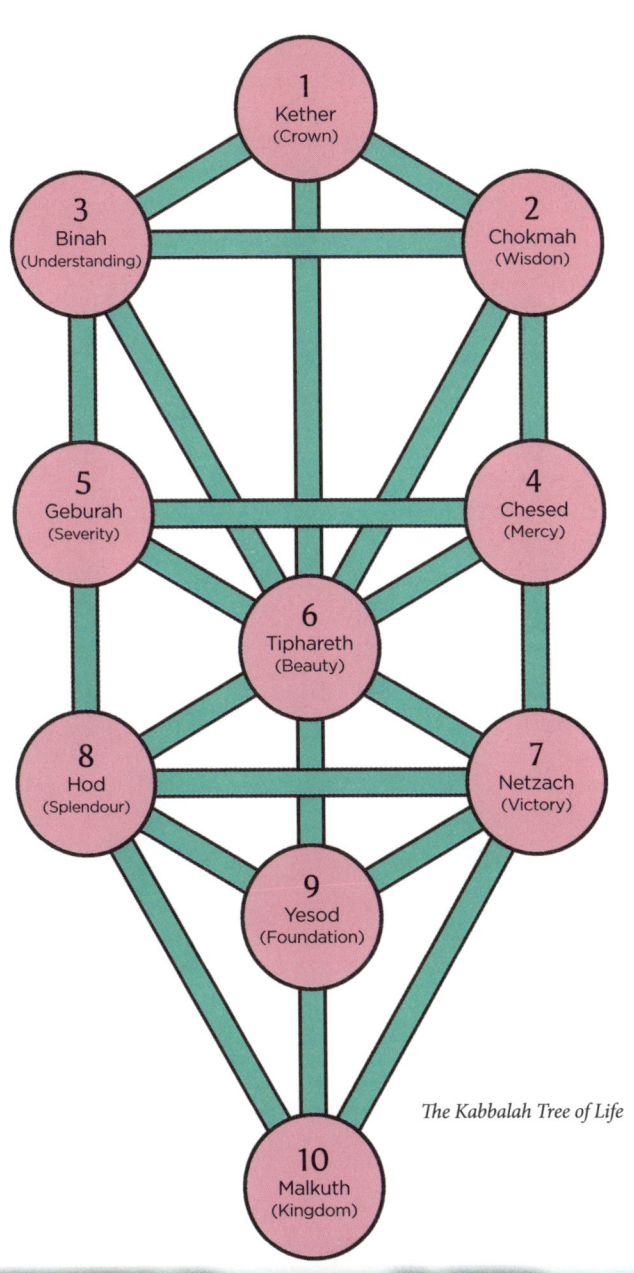

The Kabbalah Tree of Life

CHAPTER 2

to pass from one to the next – ultimately leading back to God or the creator of all.

These paths each correspond to one of the 22 letters in the Hebrew alphabet. The Hebrew alphabet is regarded as a crucial cosmic code or blueprint. The significance of the Hebrew alphabet is frequently referred to in the 13th-century Zohar (Book of Splendour), and many Jewish visionaries have emphasized that mastering the Hebrew alphabet enables one to achieve supreme knowledge of the material world.

However, in Kabbalah numerology the range of these vibrations goes up to 400, where each vibration highlights the wisdom and knowledge that the soul and mind acquire along the journey. Additionally, as opposed to the tangible physical world, these vibrations exist in the non-physical realm. The spheres are known as Sephirot, and refer to the 10 characteristics of 'Ein Sof' (the Infinite), who continuously creates both the material world and the higher metaphysical realms.

These paths all line up with one of the locations of the spheres on the Tree of Life. For instance, Kether (the Crown) is at the top and Malkuth (the Kingdom) is at the bottom of the chart. Placing Kether at the top represents the idea that Kether is the initial or fundamental link between God and the world. Malkuth, the supreme Sephirot, on the other hand, symbolizes the culmination or outcome of all the other spheres, which is the manifestation of humanity in the material world, the material cosmos, and everything that it consists of.

NUMEROLOGICAL INTERPRETATIONS

Keywords of the cycle from 1 to 10 are described as follows:

1 Kether (Crown): Progress, beginnings, development, leadership

2 Chokmah (Wisdom): Expansion, harmony, cooperation, connection

3 Binah (Understanding): Creativity, love expression, optimism

4 Chesed (Mercy): Practicality, stagnation, limitations, lack of fortune

5 Geburah (Severity): Creation, fertility, change, freedom

6 Tiphareth (Beauty): Result, execution, fulfilment, family, friendship, caring

7 Netzach (Victory): Spirit, mysticism, enlightenment, magic and mystery

8 Hod (Splendour): Impulse, abundance, success, luck, charisma

CHAPTER 2

9 Yesod (Foundation): Fortune, completion, humanitarianism, service, selflessness

10 Malkuth (Kingdom): The manifestation, final result in the physical world

To obtain your Kabbalah life-path number, use your full name given at birth, and refer to the alphanumeric chart given on page 42. Include first, middle and last names, This is because the name we are given at birth holds great energetic significance. It is a part of our soul print, our unique vibration present when we entered this lifetime. Next, divide that sum by 9 – the number of completing the cycle in numerology – and then add 1 to that number. For example, if your name Vera Claire James, then the sum of your alpha numerals are:
(4 + 5 + 9 + 1) + (3 + 3 + 1 + 9 + 5) + (1 + 1 + 4 + 5 + 1) = 19 + 21 + 12 = **52**

Next divide 52 by 9 = 5.7. Round off the number to the nearest whole number, which is 6. Finally, add 1 to it to arrive at the Kabbalah life-path number which is seven: 6 +1 = 7.

Your journey of self-discovery, learning and integration can start once you have your final number. What is your Kabbalah name number? Make of a note of it here _____.

To expand on the above essential vibrational meanings, the Tree of Life describes the path to enlightenment, or self-realization. The first three numbers address the concept that is beginning to form in the mind. The emotional component of an

idea's assessment or evaluation is what the next three numbers are focused on. The last three numbers, or steps in the cycle, represent activity that gives the concept tangible form in the real world. Malkuth, the final number, represents the manifestation.

1. Kether, The Crown

This stands for spiritual transcendence or the experience of oneness. *Kether*, which means crown, is placed above the other Sefirot in the same way that a crown is placed on top of the head. It is the first step, or the initiation.

Numerological interpretation of number 1: This stands for new beginnings, initiation and primordial power – what gave rise to everything. People with Kabbalah number 1 become outstanding leaders who put their intelligence and ingenuity to work for the greater good. These people are well-positioned and powerful in society, and they are creative and innovative.

2. Chokmah, Wisdom

It represents active intellect, the potential of what is. It is commonly thought to express the masculine or paternal principle. It represents the original idea, the 'first flash of intellect', in which all the nuances of an idea are contained but not yet defined. It is everything in its potential, like a dot, which contains everything but has yet to be actualized or defined.

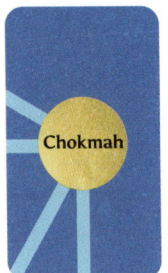

Numerological interpretation of number 2: Number 2 signifies the initial step's development and progress. It denotes

collaboration, teamwork, cooperation and community. If this is your life-path number, working in a collaborative, productive and mutually respected environment with others is best to help you achieve your goals. You also cherish community ideals and are a lover of peace and harmony, which makes you an excellent mediator, diplomat, negotiator and in service of caring or counselling others.

3. Binah, Intelligence, understanding

Passive intellect. *Binah* means to comprehend or extract one matter from another. The initial concept is broadened and deepened by Binah, becoming more crystallized and distinct than it was in the Chokmah, when the idea was vague. The previous thought, which was only a condensed version, is thus revealed and comprehended. It indicates that the dot, which stands for the feminine or mother element, has grown in both breadth and length.

Numerological interpretation of number 3: This is a wonderfully creative number and life path to have. It traditionally stands for the articulation of ideas and thoughts. If this is your life-path number, then you have inherent creative and expressive potential. Success and accomplishment are yours. The arts and creative fields frequently go hand in hand with number 3. Additionally, those with this life-path number are articulate, goal-oriented, communicative, successful entrepreneurs and artistically inclined.

4. Chesed, love, kindness

Active emotion. It symbolizes celestial benevolence and heavenly mercy and majesty. *Chesed*, which translates as loving-kindness, is the quality that freely extends kindness

and love to everyone. Creation is viewed as a manifestation of Chesed. Additionally, it alludes to the manifestation of *Shefa,* or plenty and healing. Chesed, a divine characteristic, is a term used to describe how expansion works.

Numerological interpretation of number 4: This number is incredibly practical and grounded. This could indicate stagnation or that more effort is required to reach one's goals in life. Playing to your strengths – practicality, rationality and methodology – would still make your life enjoyable, nevertheless. Life path 4 is very physically grounded, responsible and organized. It is likewise endowed with creativity and sensuality, but these qualities are grounded in physical reality and structures.

5. Geburah, the power, strength

Passive emotion. Given its capacity to constrain and contract, this number is a symbol of strength, judgment, law, authority and power. Number 5 restricts, controls and limits the flow of energy whereas Chesed, number 4, generates an outpouring of energy, maintaining a balance between expansion and contraction.

NUMEROLOGICAL INTERPRETATIONS

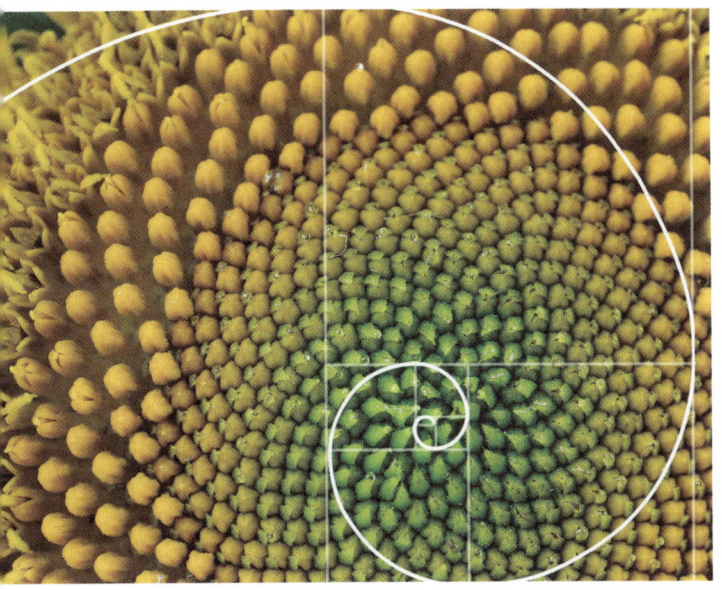

Numerological interpretation of number 5: This is the path of exploration, freedom, and freedom of expression. Success is the most important factor to you. You like to engage with all that truly impassions your heart and fires your soul. You have a lovely, compassionate heart and soul, and are passionate about your interests. This number is associated with the inner child and creativity, as well as music, singing, dancing, culture, philosophy, community and travel. According to Kabbalistic numerology, you would be most successful in life if you followed your passion and stayed true to your wild, free but beautiful heart.

6. Tiphareth, beauty, compassion

The individual self. *Tiphareth* is the midpoint of the direct line flowing down from Kether to Malkuth on the Tree of Life, and hence is positioned on the tree's central balancing column. It is also known as *Rachamim*, which means 'mercy' or 'compassion' in Hebrew. Number 6, or the sphere of Tiphareth, falls midway on the path to mystical enlightenment, between the realm of everyday existence and the reality of ultimate spiritual transcendence. It represents the fusion of Chesed and Geburah to realize its main goal, which is to promote human development to the fullest extent possible.

Numerological interpretation of number 6: The life-path number 6 represents a person who is compassionate, nurturing and community-minded. If this is your life-path number, you are likely to be sympathetic, considerate and perceptive of other people's needs. Those with the life-path number 6 may be sensitive, and like 'healing' others, because they are their most authentic selves when helping others. A counsellor, care provider, spiritual teacher or healer, therapist, holistic practitioner, community support worker, charity worker, animal or earth advocate are all good occupations to choose from. Considering that this number vibrates with empathy, understanding and compassionate connection, it also has a very powerful psychic element.

NUMEROLOGICAL INTERPRETATIONS

7. Netzach (victory)

Active action. Although the word *Netzach* is traditionally translated as 'eternity', it also refers to perpetuity, winning, endurance, conquering and overcoming in the context of Kabbalah. The idea of supremacy is thus intended to be reflected in Netzach. For instance, when you give ceaselessly, the recipient feels overwhelmed, which results in victory. It is viewed as a continuation of Chesed (number 4).

CHAPTER 2

Numerological interpretation of number 7: The number 7 is associated with mysticism, magic and enlightenment. It stands for spiritual enlightenment, discovering your inner light, and raising your level of consciousness. If you are on this life path, you are probably drawn to esotericism, metaphysics, philosophy and spirituality. You have a thorough comprehension of spiritual rules. Despite having an introverted and sensitive disposition, people with the personality number 7 show support via deeds rather than words or feelings. Additionally, they openly express their recognition of others and their talents and skills – a really powerful life path to have.

8. Hod, splendour or majesty

Passive action. *Hod* is the opposite of Netzach (number 7) and is considered to be a continuation of Geburah (5) since it represents a condition of intense tension that eventually leads to submission. Hod, which means 'thank you', 'admit' or 'submit', is derived from the Hebrew word *Hodaah*.

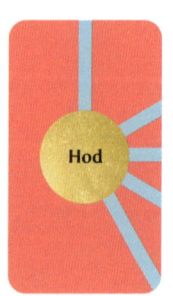

Numerological interpretation of number 8: The ethos of the number 8 life-path number is this: success is yours to enjoy if you work hard consistently and stay balanced between spirituality and materialism. In other words, you will be guided by yielding to Divine Will. That is the strain of number 8, as the scales of justice are delicate. You can lose your balance with just one step or decision in the wrong direction. The opposite is also true: recovery can be quick with the right action. It is seen as a karmic number, a lucky number, and the number of abundance and swift fruition as well as sudden loss. As long as you are committed, put in the effort and work hard, luck will work in your favour.

9. Yesod, foundation

Ego identity. *Yesod* is thought to mirror the world's foundation by promoting communication. It balances the Netzach and Hod. It relates to the soul's ability or power to interact, connect and communicate with the outside world, which is the next sphere of Malkuth. It is the bridging 'rod' that unites or grounds with the material world, or Malkuth.

Numerological interpretation of number 9: Achieving a healthy state and not losing one's identity, sense of self, or own happiness and success while also guiding and supporting others is symbolized by this life-path number, which also represents the completion of the growth cycle. People with life-path number 9 are extremely kind, generous and content to spend their lives contributing to a better world. They value integrity and are selfless: their ego is restrained. A person with life-path number 9 is a humanitarian who is dedicated to a higher purpose in life beyond materialistic goals.

10. Malkuth, The Kingdom, sovereignty, Earth

The manifestation of creation. In Hebrew it means 'kingdom', and is also the word for foundation. It is the summation of all the numbers, or spheres, that precede it. It symbolizes the end result of one's labour and the ultimate revelation of the entire creation process. It is referred to as 'having nothing of her own' in the Kabbalah. The book of Zohar compares it to the Moon, which emits light but has none of its own. Malkuth is manifested by all the spheres emerging together; it is both the recipient and the result of giving.

Numerological interpretation of number 10: As with contemporary and traditional Pythagorean numerological interpretation, Kabbalah name numerology only goes up to number 9, since $1 + 0 = 1$. While strictly speaking there may not be a life-path number 10, number 10 is still thought of as the final manifestation or outcome of the cycle from 1 to 9 in the Kabbalah. On a higher manifest and integrated level, it marks the start of a new cycle, where the zero amplifies the attributes of number 1. The vibration of life-path number 1 is reinforced by the presence of zero in the number 10.

The Jewish Kabbalah, according to scholars John Woodland Welch and Donald W. Parry, authors of *The Tree of Life: From*

CHAPTER 2

Eden to Eternity (Deseret Book, 2011), has its roots in the two mystical Kabbalah books *The Bahir* and *The Zohar*. The former appeared in the 1st century; the latter was published in the Middle Ages. Moreover, the idea of a Tree of Life with several spheres representing facets of reality had its roots in Assyria in the 9th century BC. The later Jewish Kabbalah ascribed valuations and numerical values to their gods, and the Assyrians did the same.

The Pythagoreans concluded that 'all things are numbers,' which means that everything in the cosmos can be measured, characterized and described in numbers; the odd and the even are principles of all things. The odd is limited and the even is unlimited. To this day, anytime we encounter a combined number in numerology, we reduce its numerical value to a single digit, as the Pythagoreans did, by adding the numbers together. For instance, 16 becomes 7 by adding 1 + 6.

NUMEROLOGICAL INTERPRETATIONS

You can see on the alphanumeric table (see page 42), which is used to calculate life-path numbers, that it is based on numbers 1-9, because the tenth letter in the alphabet falls under number 1 (and not 10), which reduces the sum of numbers to a single digit. Daniel Heydon wrote in *The Little Giant Encyclopaedia of Numerology* (Sterling Publishing Co. Inc New York, 2005), 'this may be a strange way to treat a number, but the practice is as old as numbers themselves and dates back to Arabia'. The purpose was to locate the root digit from whence a larger number originated in a process of ninefold progression. What becomes evident is that, since the beginning of recorded time, people in various cultures have tried to understand the world we through numbers.

The Kabbalah is a set of esoteric teachings meant to explain the relationship between the unchanging, eternal God – the mysterious Ein Sof, the Infinite – and the mortal, finite universe (God's creation). It has influenced various of schools of thought during the Enlightenment movement of the 18th century and filtered into astrology, Tarot, perhaps even Jungian psychology as well the vibrational meaning of numbers.

In the next chapter, we examine how numerology and life-path numbers can shed some insights on your own path of self-discovery.

CHAPTER 3
Numerology Readings

CHAPTER 3

Numerology considers that your life was planned prior to your birth. Numbers from your name and birthdate explain your fundamental nature, your pathway to success, your challenges, your gifts and what you came here to do. While we each have our life path to follow and life purpose to fulfil, as a soul we came here to evolve, develop and fulfil our potential in each lifetime. Numerology operates on that premise.

Your birthdate, for example, initiates a new developmental cycle. It reflects what your soul is focused on, during this lifetime, to fulfil its plan. Furthermore, a numerology reading can combine name and birthdate numerology for an in-depth look into your fundamental essence, who you are, and what your soul journey is about (for name numerology, please refer to the earlier alphanumeric table, page 42).

When you examine numbers thoroughly, their relationships to one another, which numbers are prominent or repeated, and which ones are missing, a life-path narrative begins to emerge. Especially when it comes to family numerology or compatibility numerology, numbers can reveal the intricacies of relationships as well as the purpose behind 'souls' coming into a certain family or forming relationships.

CHAPTER 3

Moreover, even if two people have the same life-path number, their inner makeup, gifts and challenges can be quite different. This is because numerology also considers your personality, your name or how you express your identity in the material world. A numerology reading provides practical guidance on a soul level as well insights that can guide you in everyday matters.

NUMEROLOGY READINGS

So, when performing a numerology reading, keep a bird's-eye view of the numbers and focus on the details. Sometimes your purpose is to let go and allow what needs to happen to be so. What guides or drives your soul's life purpose through the different cycle numbers is your personal awareness – how far your personal awareness develops in a lifetime.

Additionally, keep in mind that a good numerology reading should make sense and provide insights to empower the seeker. It is not a good idea to forewarn or anticipate the tragedies of others, because we all have free choice and a life purpose to fulfil. So, when reading for others, strive to inspire, empower and advise, but never instil any negativity. If you do, you might be influencing their will and leading them down a negative, powerless life path.

Above all, clear your mind by meditating or setting an intention, breathe deeply and let go of any preconceived ideas about the person whom you are reading for, including yourself! You may wish to light a tealight candle to help you stay focused on the information you are about to receive from numbers.

The cards enclosed in this pack can work in many different ways. You can use them to draw one a week and connect more profoundly with the numbers and their meanings before you do readings for others. You can also shuffle the cards and select one to answer a particular question you have about your life. Remember that some cards are secondary, if they can be added up to another number, apart from Master Numbers.

CHAPTER 3

Numerology Reading Template

A birthdate is broken down into three parts: green, blue and red circles, which represent birth day, birth month, and birth year, respectively. The green circle on the right represents the day of your birth and your special personality traits, as well as the underlying influences that came from your birth mother's side.

In addition, the red circle to the right of your birth month, which represents your birth year, contains the underlying vibrations that affect your life path and are 'inherited' from your birth father's side. Your primary or core vibration – also known as your core essence – is reflected in the month of your birth.

On page 124, you are shown in more detail how your birth-force number is worked out. The top triangle shows the results of adding your reduced birth day and month (which is also the personality number) together, followed by adding your birth month and year, which forms the number in the yellow circle on the right-hand side.

The desires, talents and abilities' potential – as well as what a person hopes to achieve in this lifetime – are indicated by the numbers in the top triangle. Finally, the yellow star is the sum of the single (reduced) digits from the two yellow circles, and represents the soul's ultimate yearning.

The bottom triangle is derived by subtracting the single digits of the birthday components: the green and blue, and

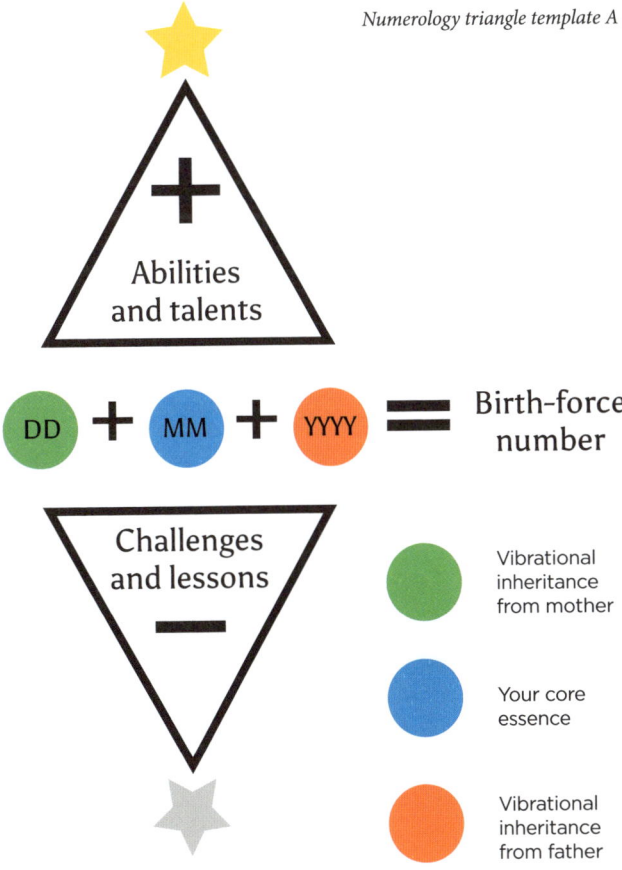

Numerology triangle template A

CHAPTER 3

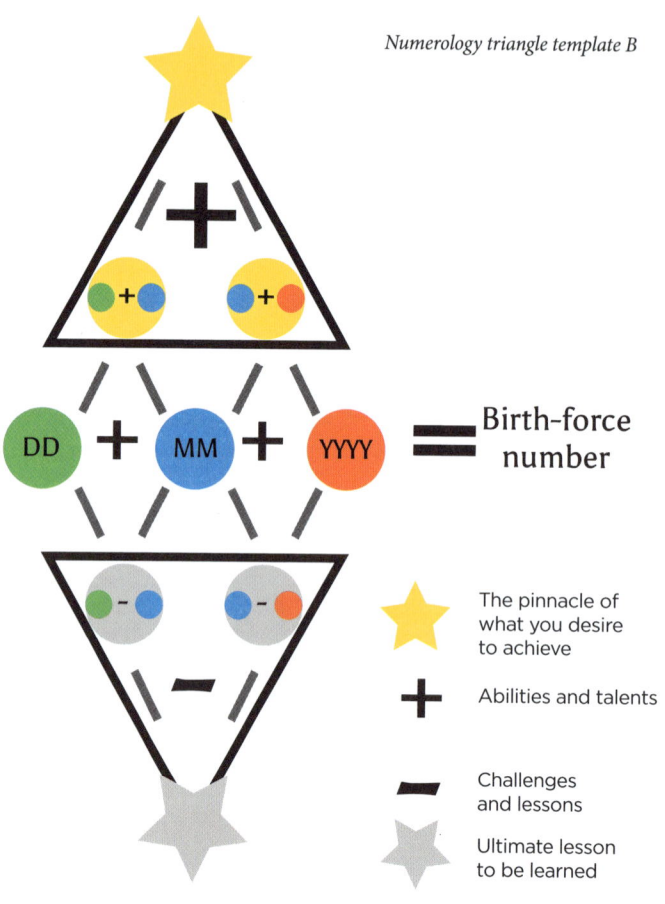

Numerology triangle template B

then the blue and red circles (single digits). Numbers in the lower triangle reflect the challenges one needs to overcome – karmic challenges vibrating from both birth parents at birth. Birth parents are thought of as the vehicle through which the soul travels, and they represent the lessons a person must learn in order to achieve their goals and live out their life's purpose (the top triangle). The grey star represents the ultimate challenge or theme to overcome.

As vibrational qualities and characteristics, the numbers in both triangles do not reflect the actual relationship one had with one's birth parents. They represent what the consciousness, or soul, is influenced by at birth from both parents. As such, any talents or abilities not expressed by either parent before your birth are 'passed on' to you and the greater is your desire to express that potential. Additionally, any challenges or lessons not learned by either parent will have an underlying influence on the challenges and lessons your soul plans to overcome. Inherited karma, if you will! Our ultimate challenge and purpose as consciousness is to express our fullest potential, whatever that may be for each of us, as the birth-force number will indicate.

Once you work out your birth-force number (or indeed one for someone you are reading for), pick out the card that represents the number and look up its meaning for greater insight into what this number, and indeed card, is telling you about your life and how to navigate it. Enjoy this multi-layered journey that numbers will take you on!

CHAPTER 3

Using this triangle template allows to easily identify:

* Birth-force, or life-path, number: the sum of your birthdate digits

* Birthday number: the sum of the day of the month on which you were born

* Birth-month number, which is your core essence: your birth month reduced to one digit

* First-impression number, which is the sum of your birth day and month. It also hints at how your life path will lay out, and what you want to fulfil

* Influences and inner gifts from ancestors (yellow circles)

* Next phase of development as one matures (numbers in the yellow and grey circles on page 124)

* Your ultimate life goal, the yellow star

- ✶ Challenges inherited from ancestors (the grey circles)

- ✶ Your ultimate lesson they came to learn (the grey star)

Name numerology adds:

- ✶ Inner-soul number (soul-urge number): sum of numbers corresponding to vowels of the full name

- ✶ Character number (outer-personality number): sum of numbers corresponding to consonants in a full name

- ✶ Expression number (destiny number): sum of all numbers corresponding to all letters of a name

Further Reading

Divine Proportion: Φ (Phi) in Art, Nature, and Science,
P. Hemenway, (Sterling Publishing Co., New York 2005)

The Little Giant Encyclopaedia of Numerology, Daniel Heydon
(Sterling Publishing Co., New York 2005)

The Numerology Kit (paperback), Carol Adrienne Plume
(Dutton Signet, 1988).

Tarot for Self-transformation: Your Journey to Happiness Mapped Out, Sahar Huneidi Palmer (Arcturus Publishing, 2022).